Trumpty Dumpty
Invades Mother Goose

"...one of the strongest supports for our democracy today comes from those of us who are seriously joking."

S. McClennen and R. Maisal, *Is Satire Saving Our Nation? Mockery and American Politics*, Palgrave MacMillan, 2014

"In the United States of America, satire is protected speech, even if the object of the satire doesn't get it."

Al Franken, as quoted in "The Trump Era Is Al Franken's Time to Shine" by Graham Vyse, in *New Republic* (2 February 2017)

I

Trumpty Dumpty
Invades Mother Goose

A Parody Is On The Loose,
Trump's Invaded Mother Goose;
A Chronicle Of Trumpty Times
Reimagined In Classic Rhymes

by Michael S. Luzzi

BOGGS HILL BOYS PRESS
Newtown. CT

© 2018 by Michael S. Luzzi

Front and back cover illustrations by *Jon Alderfer*
Interior illustrations by *Peter Aspinwall*
Front and back cover design and interior layout by *Lee Gorman*
Front cover subtitle rhyme by *Deborah Mungavin*
Author photo by *Cornelia Luzzi*

ISBN: 978-1-7321283-2-3

Printed in the United States of America

BOGGS HILL BOYS PRESS
173 Boggs Hill Road
Newtown, CT 06470

INTRODUCTION

The writing of *Trumpty Dumpty Invades Mother Goose* was an unplanned blessing. Working on it these past eight months has kept me sane (relatively speaking) as the world turned ... inside out and upside down!

In my mind, November 8, 2016 has joined the ranks of November 22, 1963, and September 11, 2001 as a singular tragedy of epic proportions. I refer to this as "The Dark American Triad." The election of Donald Trump as President of the United States was a heart-stopping, life-altering moment, which has become a recurring nightmare.   It was an event that has threatened to tear the fabric of this country apart – thread by slender thread - until there is nothing left but a democracy in shreds: The United States of America. I felt betrayed.

It just didn't make sense! Chaos reigned on network TV, on social media, and in living rooms around the country. The fear was palpable and permanence turned precarious. We were on our way to what Lincoln had warned against - "A house divided….." No one had anything insightful or philosophical to say about what took place; not the political pundits, not the Trump campaign, not even the candidate himself! Virtually no one expected him to win. The sense of safety I had become accustomed to as an American citizen vanished abruptly.

All of the countless questions could be boiled down collectively into one succinct query: What Happened? Hillary Clinton's post-election memoir used those exact words on the cover - not as a question, but rather a declarative sentence, implying the missing words, "This is …" from her title.

Thank God for the monologues of the late night comedians who took on all of the increasingly incomprehensible political events as they unfolded, dressed them up in the irony that fit best, and presented news to viewers that was (and continues to be) historically accurate and hilarious at the same time. Satire at its best.

I woke up – literally and figuratively – on a beautiful sunny morning in the middle of June 2017, and said out loud, "This really did happen! It isn't going away any time soon…" Six months had gone by and I was stuck in the fourth stage grief: Depression. Writing letters to the editor and sparring with trolls on Facebook was not comforting and did nothing to heal the hole in my heart.

At that point, I recognized something about myself that was truly frightening: My no-holds-barred sense of humor had gone missing. Irony had been my friend; I could find humor in just about anything – especially absurdity. And nothing was more incongruous than Donald Trump being the president.

My spirit felt like it had been broken into pieces - like many other Americans, - so many pieces, in fact, there was a question of whether or not the country could ever be put back together again? Wait a minute… That phrase sounded very familiar. Hence, the birth and evolution of *Trumpty Dumpty.*

As I referenced earlier, working on this has tempered my own outrage and frustration and has prevented the dark shadow of pessimism from eclipsing what I have long referred to as an incurable idealism. I had to accept this alternate reality, but certainly wasn't about to do so passively. This book is an example of my active resistance to the spectacle our government and nation have become.

The fact that I chose characters and stories from Mother Goose nursery rhymes as archetypes to epitomize Trumpty & Co.turned out to be serendipitous. The backstory and basis of many of these original classics are dark and have derived from harsh treatment of the general populace by greedy and unpopular rulers.The links at the end of this introduction will reveal just how relevant this metaphor really is.When Trumpty took office, he even came in with his own wall....

http://abckidsinc.com/mother-goose-nursery-rhymes-meanings/

http://www.bbc.com/culture/story/20150610-the-dark-side-of-nursery-rhymes

TABLE OF CONTENTS

Dedicated to my incredible wife, Cornelia, and my sons, Nicholas and Morgan, who illuminate my life and continue to make it possible for me to express love and find humor in this upside-down world.

Trumpty Dumpty *via Humpty Dumpty*

Trumpty Dumpty insisted, "A Wall!"
He never imagined how far he would fall.
For all of his bluster, flag waving and pomp,
Trumpty's now sweating a trip to his swamp

New Oath Of Office *via Old Mother Hubbard*

The New Oath of Office
Made everyone cautious
It gave the poor country a scare

As Trump spoke each word
They all sounded absurd
Like he wasn't even there.

Trumpty Dumpty *via Humpty Dumpty*
(The Inauguration)

Trumpty Dumpty stood on the dais
Trumpty said only he could save us
But all of his lackeys and all of his wealth
Couldn't even save Trumpty from himself

Surly To Bed *via Early To Bed*

Surly to bed,
Churly to rise,
Makes a fool hide
In a man's disguise,
Makes that man tweet
Incredible lies!

Are You Tweeting *via Brother John*

Are you tweeting? Are you tweeting?
Trumpty Don, Trumpty Don!
While the world is working.
Your tweeter feed is lurking
With fake news,
The latest ruse!

Vlad & Don *via Jack & Jill*

Vlad and Don, they shared a bong
And up the hill they stumbled.
Don soon moaned, "I'm really stoned!"
And down the hill he tumbled.

Don cried, "Vlad, I'm hurt real bad!"
Vlad waved, said, "Don, don't worry."
Pulled out his cell, said, "Trump fell,
Lot of blood...but don't hurry."

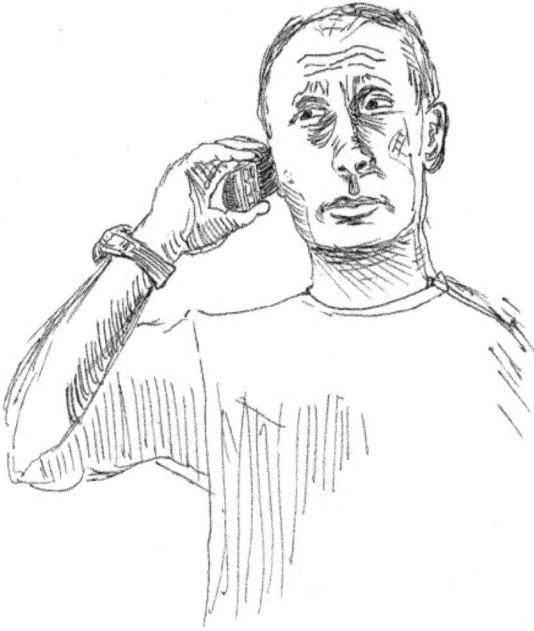

I'm An Orange Crackpot *via I'm A Little Teapot*

I'm an orange crackpot
I'm not stout
No limb is tiny
There's no doubt
If you criticize me
I will pout
Tweet you a pink slip
And you are out!

A Blob Went Debatin' *via A Frog Went A-Courtin'*

A Blob went-debatin' he did lie, aha
A Blob went-debatin' he did lie, aha
A Blob went-debatin' he did lie,
Ignored the truth didn't bat an eye
Aha, Aha, Aha

He strode behind as Hillary talked, aha
He strode behind as Hillary talked, aha
He strode behind as Hillary talked,
Couldn't compete so he just stalked
Aha, Aha, Aha

Benghazi this and Benghazi that, aha
Benghazi this and Benghazi that, aha
Benghazi this and Benghazi that,
He's just a lyin' plutocrat
Aha, Aha, Aha

The Blob resorted to email claims, aha
The Blob resorted to email claims, aha
The Blob resorted to email claims,
Further proof that he had no game
Aha, Aha, Aha

Challenged Barack Obama's birth, aha
Challenged Barack Obama's birth, aha
Challenged Barack Obama's birth,
Denied we're heatin' up the earth
Aha, Aha, Aha

The Blob ended up as president, aha
The Blob ended up as president, aha
The Blob ended up as president,
The lamest White House resident
Aha, Aha, Aha

But, we the people are on his case, aha
Yes, we the people are on his case, aha
With Mueller's evidence in his face,
The Blob will resign in disgrace
Aha, Aha, Aha

Where Have You Been Roger Stone? *via Billy Boy*

Oh, where have you been,
Roger Stone, Roger Stone?
Oh, where have you been,
Raging Roger?
I have been with Alex Jones,
Some folks think that we are clones,
We're obnoxious
And cannot leave each other.

Did he ask you on his show,
Roger Stone, Roger Stone?
Did you go on InfoWars,
Hateful Roger?
Yes, he bade me to appear,
You know, given my career,
We would help Trump
Cuz he was like our brother.

Was the Donald pleased as pie,
Roger Stone, Roger Stone?
Was he sure that you would lie,
Shifty Roger?
He was thrilled that me and Jones
Had double-dealing in our bones,
He said you guys
Are just like one another.

Do you have any regrets,
Roger Stone, Roger Stone?
Are you happy with yourself,
Shameless Roger?
Lucky for the Trump campaign
InfoWars was not in vain
Jones and I both
Were raised without a mother.

NoFair Donald Has A Barn *via Old MacDonald*

NoFair Donald has a barn, E-I-E-I-O
And in his barn he has a staff, E-I-E-I-O
With a white guy here and a white girl there
Here it's white, there it's white
Everywhere it's whitewhite
NoFair Donald has a barn, E-I-E-I-O

NoFair Donald has a barn, E-I-E-I-O
And in his barn he tweets the Press, E-I-E-I-O
With "fake news" here and "not true" there
Here it's fake, there it's false
Everywhere it's wrongwrong
NoFair Donald's gonna sue, E-I-E-I-O

NoFair Donald has a barn, E-I-E-I-O
And in his barn he signs his name, E-I-E-I-O
With no health plan and no clean air
Here we die, there we choke
Everywhere this man's a joke
NoFair Donald doesn't care, E-I-E-I-O
CONTROVERSY EVERYWHERE, **E-I-E-I-O-O-O**

Itsy-Bitsy Betsy *via Itsy-Bitsy Spider*

Itsy-Bitsy Betsy has won a Cabinet post
Of all the nominations, this one hurts the most
At her Senate hearing, Franken asked a Q
"Growth vs. Proficiency?" She clearly had no clue

Thrown a softball question, Devos's face just paled
Itsy Bitsy Betsy: on her first test she failed
TV cameras rolling, recording our worst fears
The senator was wide-eyed, could not believe his ears

Despite her poor performance, she was confirmed posthaste
But Itsy Bitsy Betsy thinks public school's a waste
Head of Education, our children are at stake
How could this position have gone to such a flake?

Vouchers, vouchers everywhere, vouchers every day
Itsy-Bitsy Betsy, we wish you'd go away.

Ding-Dong Donald *via Good Morning To You*

Good morning to you,
Good morning to you,
We're all in our places
To go through the paces
And all do our best
To bow to Trump's quest
Good morning, dear leader our Liege
(We'll help you continue your siege…)

Good morning to you,
Good morning to you,
Pence opted to go first
His speech so well rehearsed
So honored to serve you
Though we don't deserve you
Good morning, my pride's out the door
(Just tell me if I could do more…)

Good morning to you,
Good morning to you,
It's me, AG Sessions
To give my impressions
Of how great it feels
To lap at your heels
Good morning, how grateful I am
(To help make this country a sham…)

Good morning to you,
Good morning to you,
It's Tom Price, I'm happy
To gush and be sappy
Whatever you ask
No matter the task
Good morning, sir, I'm such a fan
(I no longer act like a man...)

Good morning to you,
Good morning to you,
It's Chief of Staff, Priebus
We love how you lead us
We'll all do our duty
Include kiss your booty
Good morning, we promise each day
(Whatever the price, we will pay...)

Good morning to you,
Good morning to you,
The TV crews gather
To film all this blather
The fools at this table
Creating a fable
Good morning, it's beyond belief
(Good God, will you please give relief...)

Don's Nullify *via Brahm's Lullaby*

Nullify, say goodnight
With Red allies take flight
With falsehoods o'er spread
On our President's thick head
Step you down now, it's best
May our future be blessed
Step you down now, it's best
May our future be blessed

Nullify, please take flight
You're our dear nation's blight
Darkest demons beside
Our fake President abide
Stark and bare is your bed
Stop those tweets, sleep instead
Stark and bare is your bed
Stop those tweets, sleep instead

Sleepless fool, close your eyes
There is no one beside you
No protection, no spinning
So forget about winning
Sycophants are not near
So sleep on, face your fear
Sycophants are not near
So sleep on, face your fear

Nullify, make it right
Hush, our Nightmare is sleeping
On his sheets, black as tar
Dreaming golf, making par
When he wakes around noon
Be impeached none too soon
When he wakes around noon
He can tweet a new tune

Baa Baa Donald *via Baa Baa Black Sheep*

Baa Baa Donald
Have you any bull?
Yes sir, the best sir
Used to pull the wool

Some for the media
Known as fake news
One for my lawyer
In case anyone sues

Some for the voters
All the red states
Duped to elect me
They sealed their fates

And some for the sycophants -
The white house staffs
Humiliated daily
To cover my gaffes

Oh pseudo-president
Have you any bull?
Believe me, the best sir
A twitter-trove full...

No King Cole *via Old King Cole*

No King Cole was a man without soul
And a narcissist was he,
Trump was called "The Chief"
Thought the U.S. was his Fief
And demanded complete fealty.

Every Cabinet member had a task
Some even had two or three,
But nothing could compare
With his focus on his hair
And all his sentences ending with "me."

Re-mind Spice *via Three Blind Mice*

Re-mind Spice, Re-mind Spice,
Where did he run? Why did he shun
The press who wait on the White House Lawn,
To ask about why James Comey's gone?
Did you ever see such sheer snobbery?
A grown man who hid in the shrubbery?
Re-mind Spice, that's just not nice.

A Golf Club, A Golf Pro *via A Tisket, A Tasket*

A golf club, a golf pro
I'm off to Mar-A-Lago
As President, I tweet all week
Weekends are for quid pro quo
Quid pro,
Quo pro,
Yes, what that means, I don't know?
The media will pick it up
Air it on a fake news show

Donnie Had Some Little Hands *via*
Mary Had a Little Lamb

Donnie had some little hands,
Little hands, little hands
Donnie had some little hands
Small fingers, tiny toes.
And everywhere he put his hands,
Put his hands, put his hands
Everywhere he put his hands
Was anywhere he chose.

They followed him to work one day,
Work one day, work one day
He brought them into work each day
Attached below his arms.
Bannon said put those away,
Those away, those away
Told him, "Use your pockets, sir
Where they will do no harm."

Donnie said, "But I'm the Prez,
I'm the Prez, I'm the Prez
And because I am the Prez
Don't tell me what to do!"
Kushner said, "But Bannon's right,
Bannon's right, Bannon's right
Someone has to tell you, sir
Because you have no clue."

Donnie frowned then pursed his lips,
Pursed his lips, pursed his lips
Fiddled with his fingertips
Then plunked down on the floor.
He crossed his arms and stomped his feet,
Stomped his feet, stomped his feet
He said, "Don't make me send a tweet
Cuz I can start a war!"

Ivanka said, "I've got a plan,
Got a plan, got a plan
Praise his immigration ban
He'll stop this fuss and hissing.
Get his tweeter and TV,
His TV, Fox TV
Lock him in his room, you'll see
He'll never know he's missing!"

I-Dunno Was His Name *via Bingo Was His Name*

There was a U.S. president
I-Dunno was his name-O
D-U-N-N-O
D-U-N-N-O
D-U-N-N-O
I-Dunno was his name-O

To Clinton he cried, "Lock Her Up!"
"She's crooked" was his claim-O
C-L-A-I-M
C-L-A-I-M
C-L-A-I-M
"She's crooked" was his claim-O

I-Dunno was short on facts
He lied himself to fame-O
L-Y-I-N-G
L-Y-I-N-G
L-Y-I-N-G
He lied himself to fame-O

He had some issues with non-whites
A bigot with no shame-O
S-H-A-M-E
S-H-A-M-E
S-H-A-M-E
A bigot with no shame-O

So irresponsible was he
He always had to blame-O
B-L-A-M-E
B-L-A-M-E
B-L-A-M-E
He always had to blame-O

There was some doubt that he would win
So Putin fueled the flame-O
P-U-T-I-N
P-U-T-I-N
P-U-T-I-N
So Putin fueled the flame-O

Trump tried to bait the FBI
But Comey knew his game-O
C-O-M-E-Y
C-O-M-E-Y
C-O-M-E-Y
But Comey knew his game-O

A special counsel has been formed
Now will the beast be tamed-O
T-A-M-E-D
T-A-M-E-D
T-A-M-E-D
Now will the beast be tamed-O?

The drumroll for Impeachment sounds
With "Lock'm Up" the aim-O
L-O-C-K-M
L-O-C-K-M
L-O-C-K-M
With "Lock'm Up" the aim-O

So, US Prez, Don I-Dunno
Becomes Inmate 4-5-Oh
INMATE 4-5-Oh
INMATE 4-5-Oh
INMATE 4-5-Oh
Will be his Badge of Shame-O
His permanent New Name-O

Climate Change Hot *via Pease Porridge Hot*

Climate Change hot,
Climate Change cold,
Climate Change is in the air
Say scientists polled
Some say it's fake, but truth be told
The earth's heating up for us to behold

Mitch McConnell *via Peter Piper*

Mitch McConnell made a mess of a medical model
A mess of a medical model, Mitch McConnell made
If Mitch McConnell made a mess of a medical model
Where's the mess of the medical model that
Mitch McConnell made?

Little Tommy Price *via Little Tommy Tucker*

Little Tommy Price, he
Turned out not so nice, he

Broke some rules in Georgia
Still allowed to forge a

Career... What did he get?
A post in Trump's cabinet:

Health and Human Service
Makes poor people nervous.

Bannon Bo Peep *via Little Bo Peep*

Bannon Bo Peep, Trump's Strategist creep
Had a racist reputation
That tag was well-earned
And now we have learned
Don sent Steve on "vacation"

It's safe to say, with Bannon away
Another bigot will be hired
Whom Trump will abuse
Then blame the fake news
For making him say, "You're fired!"

Old Uncle Sammy *via Old Mother Hubbard*

Old Uncle Sammy
Caught in a jam, he
Put Freedom high on his list.
He tried to proceed
But Trump disagreed
So Uncle Sam said: **RESIST!**

Trump-a-Dub-Dub *via Rub-a-Dub-Dub*

Trump-a-dub-dub,
Kelly at the hub
He's new Chief of Staff – What a mess!
The Spice plus The Mooch,
And Priebus cut loose,
They all jumped off the ship
Who's next is anyone's guess

Little Jeff Sessions *via Little Jack Horner*

Little Jeff Sessions made no confessions
Lied to the Senate Committee
His foot in his mouth, this troll from the
South
Is a racist, too…what a pity!

At his second hearing, hardly endearing
Overdoing his Southern drawl
Accepting no blame, refuting all claims:
Once again, "Ah do not recall."

Little Jeff Sessions answered no questions
Dishonored his prestigious post
He kept repeating, "Ah had no meeting,"
So Kislyak must be a ghost!

Scaramucci Had a Job *via Old MacDonald*

Scaramucci had a job, E-I-E-I-O
And in his job he looked for leaks, E-I-E-I-O
With a Big Mouth here
And a Reince Rat there
Here a Mouth, there a Rat
Big Mouth Reince will pay for that
Scaramucci on the case, E-I-E-I-O

Scaramucci had a job, E-I-E-I-O
And in his job he spoke a lot, E-I-E-I-O
With a Muh Muh here
And a Fuh Fuh there
Here a Muh, There a Fuh
Everywhere a Muh-Fuh
Scaramucci lost his job, E-I-E-I-O

Scaramucci had a job, E-I-E-I-O
And in his job he spent 10 days, E-I-E-I-O
With I'm da Mooch here
And you're a douche there
Here da Mooch, there a douche
Maybe Mooch is da real Douche
Moochie didn't last too long, E-I-E-I-O

Little Pence Veep *via Little Bo Peep*

Little Pence Veep, one of Trump's sheep
Keeps doing his boss's bidding
But when he's alone
He tweets on his own,
"Chief Cheeto's got to be kidding!"

When Donnie's asleep, his ambitious Veep
Imagines himself the leader
"If Congress impeaches for
Security breaches,
I will become the Chief Tweeter!"

Sing A Song Of Mike Pence *via Sing A Song Of Sixpence*

Sing a song of Mike Pence,
A pocket full of lies,
Contacts with the Russians?
Denies, denies, denies!

When it was discovered
That Flynn had lied to Pence,
Cries to investigate
Began to all make sense!

Scaramucci's Going Down *via London Bridge*

Scaramucci's going down,
Going down, going down,
Mooch behaves like such a clown,
No more chances.

Just can't keep The Mooch contained,
Mooch contained, Mooch contained,
Nothing further to be gained,
From his presence.

Even Trump cannot believe,
Not believe, not believe,
What The Mooch has up his sleeve,
What's his motive?

No one knows what Mooch is thinking,
Mooch is thinking, Mooch is thinking,
Some believe he must be drinking,
Has no censor.

Compared to Moochie, Trump had class,
Trump had class... Trump had *class?*
Not even he could be so crass,
With his language.

As I write this, Mooch is out,
Mooch is out, The Mooch is out,
No more will his foul mouth spout,
Indiscretions...

Scara-Mooch is histor-y
Histor-y, histor-y
How to write his legacy:
"@#&%$?!@)(¶$%"...

General John Kelly *via Little Jack Horner*

General John Kelly
Traveled through Hell, he
Led our troops in Iraq.
His new position?
A road to perdition
Has him wishing that he could go back.

Sarah, Sarah, Secretar-ah *via Mary, Mary, Quite Contrary*

Sarah, Sarah, Secretar-ah
How do you face the press?
With a straight face. What a disgrace!
Spouting lie after lie, no less.

Secretary, quite contrary
How does your mouth divide?
You seem to confuse spin with news
And leave it to chance to decide.

Sarah, Sarah, Secretar-ah
How do you manage to sneer?
Reporters ask questions despite your objections
Tell us, why do you think they're here?

Hey Donald-Diddle *via Hey Diddle-Diddle*

Hey Donald-Diddle, that's Trump in the middle
Of a scandal involving buffoons.
Nobody laughed to see this debacle
May the Prez go to jail with his goons.

Donnie, Donnie *via Mary, Mary*

Donnie, Donnie, quite the con, he
Couldn't a garden grow
No edible plants, no second chance
No "Apprentice President" show.

The Sad Old American Prez
via The Grand Old Duke of York

Oh, the sad old American Prez,
He assembled a faithful bunch.
He herded them into the Oval Room,
Then he chased some out to lunch.

And when they came back, they were glum,
And when they were gone, so relieved,
With no way of knowing who's coming or going,
No one knew what to believe.

Kelly CON-way *via Georgie Porgie*

Kelly CON-way couldn't not lie
Looks the camera in the eye
When the facts refute her news
She's ready with another ruse

She's been rated bad-to-worse
But CON-way needs another verse
When Kelly can't explain a leak
She lapses into Kellyspeak

Poor Georgie Porgie lost his rhyme
No kissing and no girls this time
And boys can't play, cuz
they got bumped
Georgie Porgie's rhyme
got Trumped!

Little Ms CON-way *via Little Miss Muffet*

Little Ms CON-way started each Monday
Spouting fake news to the Press.
By Friday each anchor
Fed up with her rancor
Invited her back less and less.

Little Boy You *via Little Boy Blue*

Little Boy You
Who has no horn,
And no impulse control
Since when you were born.
Who are these lackeys who look after your needs,
Who take all the flak for your misdeeds?
Puppets perhaps, Yes-men for sure;
Brown-nosers for the would-be Führer?

Will they say no?
No, not they,
For if they do,
They're sent away.

Stephen Miller *via Mary, Mary*

Stephen Miller, Trumpty's shill-
Er, How does he sleep at night?
He must sedate with dreams of hate
And fantasies of how to incite!

Stephen Miller, perfect filler:
Mouthpiece for White House lies;
What Trumpty claims, Stevie lays blame
Without any wherefores or whys

Twinkle Twinkle 50 Stars *via Twinkle Twinkle Little Star*

Twinkle twinkle 50 stars
How we hope you'll still be ours
War or peace you always stood
In every town and neighborhood
Twinkle twinkle 50 stars
How we hope you'll still be ours

Twinkle, twinkle 50 stars
Resist despots, keep out tsars
Feels like an attempted coup
Traitors seek to hijack you
Twinkle, twinkle 50 stars
How we hope you'll still be ours

Twinkle twinkle 50 stars
Our fake Prez has shown his cards
Putin and the Oligarchs
Influenced our ballot marks
Twinkle twinkle 50 stars
How we hope you'll still be ours

Twinkle twinkle 50 stars
Help us to prevent this farce
Comrade Trump so enamored
With the sickle and the hammer
Twinkle, twinkle 50 stars
Let them have him, you are ours

Moscow Swamp Is Filling Up
via London Bridge Is Falling Down

Moscow Swamp is filling up
Filling up, filling up
Moscow Swamp is filling up
With more scandals

Dam it up by coming clean
Coming clean, coming clean
Dam it up by coming clean
About the Russians

Drain the swamp and clear the air
Clear the air, clear the air
Drain the swamp now if you dare
Lying Trumpsters

"Adoption" option was a ruse
Was a ruse, was a ruse
Twisting facts is no excuse
Don't blame Clinton

Moscow swamp is filling up
Filling up, filling up
Moscow swamp is filling up
Dam is bursting!

There Was A Lame Congress
via There Was An Old Woman

There was a lame Congress
Who lived in D.C.
Partisan pinheads
Who refused to agree

So they got nothing done
As was expected
Gross disregard for
Why they were elected

There Was A Fake Leader
via There Was An Old Woman

There was a fake leader
Who lived in his head,
So much empty space there
Echoed what he said,
But he still ran his mouth off
And tweeted each day
'Til the country got fed up
And sent him away.

Clinton Had A Campaign Plan
via Mary Had A Little Lamb

Clinton had a campaign plan
Campaign plan, campaign plan
Clinton had a campaign plan
Whose message was obscured

But if her team could make it work
Make it work, make it work
If her team could make it work
Her victory was assured.

Trump followed her around the room
Around the room, around the room
He followed her around the room
Which was against the rules

He made a farce of their debates
Their debates, their debates
Trump made a farce of their debates
Because he was a fool.

But in the end, the moron won
Moron won, moron won,
In the end, the moron won
Who knew "hate" would prevail?

If there is justice in this world
In this world, in this world
If there is justice in this world
He'll end his term in jail.

EPILOGUE:

From this page up to God's ears
To God's ears, to God's ears
From this page up to God's ears
Good-bye to all this hate.

Clear the White house stem to stern
Stem to stern, stem to stern
Tell the world the worm has turned
Would be well worth the wait!

Robert Mueller Had A List *via Old MacDonald*

Robert Mueller had a list, E-I-E-I-O
And on his list he had some names, E-I-E-I-O
With a Manafort here and a Mike Flynn there
Russian collusion everywhere
Robert Mueller had a list, E-I-E-I-O

Robert Mueller had a list, E-I-E-I-O
And on that list was "Trump's Campaign" E-I-E-I-O
With a Rich Gates here, Papadopoulos there,
And Carter Page trolling everywhere
Robert Mueller had a list, E-I-E-I-O

Robert Mueller isn't done, E-I-E-I-O
Not til he's questioned everyone, E-I-E-I-O
With Priebus here and Spicer there
Kushner and Jr's lies laid bare
Special Counsel far from done, E-I-E-I-O

Robert Mueller had a plan, E-I-E-I-O
And in his plan Trump is the man, E-I-E-I-O
With subpoenas here and indictments there
Russian fingerprints everywhere
Trumpty caught in the crosshairs, E-I-E-I-O

The Charmer's In The Cell *via The Farmer in the Dell*

The Charmer's in the cell
No farmer in the dell
Hi-ho, no derry-o
This guy's a ne-er-do-well

The candidate from Hell
His wife, a Slavic belle
How he wooed Melania
She would never tell

The skinny from intel
Familiar with his sell
Fake, fraud, and ignorant
Warned those who knew him well

Right from the first debate
Was clear he couldn't wait
Hi-ho, from the get-go
His words were filled with hate

The tone of his campaign
Like venom in in the vein
Ho-hi, oh why oh why
His message was insane

Finally on that night
With victory in sight
Hi-ho, his base did grow
Democracy took flight

And then he took the oath
In his Address he quoth
Ho-hi, the biggest lie
"There'll be tremendous growth!"

The charmer tried to sell
New health care, not so well
Hi-ho a bruised ego
His polling numbers fell

Fake charm began to wane
His ego was in pain
Ho-hi, the time is nigh
To end this bigot's reign

For all the lies and tweets
Backpedals and retreats
Hi-ho, to jail he goes
We're dancing in the streets

Trumpty Dumpty: *The Year in Retrospect*

Trumpty Dumpty surprised that he won
Trumpty knew it would end all his fun
He never intended to win the race
And how we all wish that had been the case

Trumpty Dumpty puddin' and pie
He groped the girls then told a lie
When his accusers have their say
Trumpty Dumpty will have to pay

Trumpty Dumpty lived in his head
Not thinking about what he hadn't read
Not The Bill of Rights, not the Rule of Law
For Trumpty Dumpty reads nothing at all

Trumpty Dumpty lived without facts
Trumpty, for instance, paid no tax
Everything true and everything real
For Trumpty it's just The Art of the Deal

Trumpty Dumpty, Tweeter-in-Chief
His lack of knowledge was beyond belief
No interest in learning what he didn't know
Just tweeting and golfing at Mar-a-lago

Trumpty Dumpty sat on his bed
No briefings, no folders, three TVs instead
All the staff members, his family, and friends
Their advice ignored, they're at wits ends

Trumpy Dumpty sat on his ass
Trumpty Dumpty so little class
One year gone, it makes no sense
To cope with his willful incompetence

Trumpty Dumpty, Child-in-Chief
Daily tantrums and constant grief
Why does the Republic of this great land
Allow this nonsense and mayhem to stand

Trumpty Dumpty lived in a bubble
Trumpty's tweets spelled nothing but trouble
Tiny fingers on a tiny keyboard
Reminded the world of "The Mouse That Roared"

Trumpty Dumpty sat at his desk
Just kept repeating, "I'm the best!"
Or else "I'm the greatest," always "the most"
While none of it's true, he still has to boast

Trumpty Dumpty was uninvolved
Trumpty Dumpty had no resolve
Even those who cared for him most
Said mouth always open, mind always closed

Trumpty Dumpty racist for sure
But he's not the only "Bigot du jour"
There's Miller, Sessions, Bannon, and Pence
Trumpty & Co. need no pretense

Trumpty Dumpty, accuser-at-large
 Morning Joe hosts have faced this charge:
"Joe is a psycho and Mika is dumb"
Trumpty has an insult for everyone

Trumpty Dumpty, Liar-in-Chief
For Trumpty deception's his main motif
His administration has been surreal
Mastered "The Artifice of the Deal!"

Trumpty Dumpty behaved madly
Thus, his presidency went badly
His decisions varied from bad to worse
Trumpty became America's curse

Trumpty Dumpty, Putin's decoy
It's like comparing a hack to Tolstoy
All the denials and noise he would make
To keep us from knowing he's the real fake!

Trumpty Dumpty sat on a wall
Trumpty Dumpty had a great fall
All this fool's minions and court jesters too
May soon be behind bars…Well, Boo-hoo-hoo!

Trumpty Dumpty was on thin ice
Trumpty would soon have to pay the price
For behaviors that have been so abhorrent:
First, a subpoena, and then a warrant

Trumpty Dumpty *(First Anniversary-1/20/18)*
Trumpty Dumpty – one year today
Took the Oath and we've had to pay
Incompetence, danger, all year we've mourned
But no one can say we hadn't been warned

Trumpty Dumpty *via "Rock-a bye-baby"*
Trumpty Dumpty on the wall-top
Watching indictments starting to drop
When the news breaks about his downfall
It won't be just Trumpty who's knocked off that wall

CITATIONS AND ACKNOWLEDGMENTS

Citations

List of Nursery Rhymes, Alphabetically, Nurseryrhymes.org, Marin Granum, nurseryrhymes.org.

Horwich, Francis. Ding Dong School, WNBQ, Chicago, 1952. en.m.wikipedia.org.

S. McClennen and R. Maisal, *Is Satire Saving Our Nation? Mockery and American Politics,* Palgrave MacMillan, New York, 2014, ISBN: 978-1-137-42796-0.

Acknowledgments

Why this, why now? For *Trumpty Dumpty Invades Mother Goose,* why now? Because of who he is, what he has done, and what he is capable of doing. Why this? Because of the current giants and geniuses of satire, whose relentless parodies have been stabilizing and inspiring, informative and hopeful. With them I have sought refuge and found comfort every single day since 11/8/16! Their monologues and commentary have consistently helped to remove the bewilderment from political bedlam, recalibrate our BS meters, and reset our reality compasses back toward true north. So, from the bottom of my heart, I say thank you to Stephen Colbert, John Oliver, Samantha Bee, and Trevor Noah; to Seth Meyers, Jimmy Fallon, and everyone at Saturday Night Live;

to Jimmy Kimmel and Bill Maher and, last, but certainly not least, Jon Stewart. And, speaking of giants, my gratitude to "Al Franken, Giant of the Senate." I hope *Trumpty Dumpty Invades Mother Goose* passes muster with all of you.

Writing is primarily a solitary activity. The author gets top billing; the rest are relegated to "supporting cast" status. That's a pretty incomplete rendering of the process of finishing a book. Research, editing, encouragement, nourishment and love, inspiration and motivation, as well as endurance training when energy flags and frustration rises, all contribute in equal amounts. To be accurate this section should be called, Huge Gratitude and Acknowledgments because brief "thank you's" are totally inadequate... Finally, there is no particular order in which I am grateful.

My wife, Cornelia, and sons, Nicholas and Morgan, to whom this book is dedicated were, among countless other things, also my first line of readers to ring in on each rhyme as it was written. Some first drafts were frightening, but they were gentle with their criticism and generous with their support.

Friends since our college days, Lee Gorman patiently and meticulously designed the presentation and layout of the book from cover to cover; his wife, Debby Gorman, reprised her dedicated role of shepherding me through a BA in

English over 46 years ago, and rose to the occasion once again. She was intimately involved in valuable research and major editing decisions all along the way. Words of praise from her provided monumental incentive given what she knows about books, literature and the nuances of language. Equally vital were the contributions of friends-cum-family members, Nick Kourabas and Deborah Mungavin. Debbie is an artist and poet, who created the (subtitle) poem on the cover of *Trumpty Dumpty Invades Mother Goose,* and did double-duty as the titular chair of our five-person editorial committee. Nick is also a writer whose editorial insights and unique friendship kept my boat afloat, so to speak, when it threatened to be tossed by the winds of low self-esteem and crash against the sharp rocks of self-doubt.

Having one's closest friends at the ready is like having on-call medical personnel: a rendezvous, a short walk, a phone call, or a text away were those who routinely nurtured my soul, offered encouragement, inspired confidence, provided perspective, and shared love. In order of geographical proximity, love and gratitude to: Suzette LeBlanc and Paul Piazza; Phyllis and Bumper McPherson; Peter Holskin, Janice Feher, Stefanie Kihm, and Dennis Frusciano.

Inconvenient geographical proximity did not deter Marguerite and Harvey Mains from contributing "hugely" to this project. Our friends moved temporarily to France before I started writing *Trumpty Dumpty Invades Mother Goose,* but that proved to be no impediment to the support they offered. Harvey had provided much needed technological advice about what happens after you turn the computer on (that was not a joke). Friend and wizard, David Voytek, remained local and re-defined the term, tech support. Marguerite seemed to have forgotten she left the neighborhood because via texts, emails, facetime, and WhatsApp contact, she had me going in several different directions at once for helpful solutions to snags. With her proactive personality and marketing executive background, she researched small presses, self-publishing options, and devoured websites for information; in addition she recommended illustrators and sent multiple lists of independent bookstores. Many thanks.

Others with whom I shared early drafts offered encouragement and praise through their feedback. Each recommended resources for further development. I thank poet, Evelyn Augusto, my friend who, upon reading my first two *Trumpty Dumpty* rhymes, enthusiastically suggested that I write an entire book of similar poems. Also, of particular importance, she was relentless in locating the incredibly gifted artist and illustrator, Jon Alderfer whose extraordinary color illustrations appear on both the front and back covers. My sincere gratitude to: Barbara Roberts, Nancy Stauffer Cahoon, Laura Schaefer, owner of Scattered Books, Sally Champagne, and Erica Jong.

Finally, I am very grateful for the unselfish and necessary professional services of Harry Adamakos, Ph.D. and Chris Morik, J.D. Special thanks to former student and talented artist, Peter Aspinwall, who stepped up in the middle of the project with a unique style to capture the essence of the rhymes. Also essential were the miracles performed on my aging Subaru Forester by my Meineke friend, Jerry Gobindraj.

...The End of *Trumpty Dumpty*

Trumpty Dumpty, you must step down,
Trumpty, you have messed with "the crown."
There's almost no one you haven't maligned;
Bad-mouthing Oprah?! Have you lost your mind?

Really, Trumpty, you must resign,
Your recent tweet has crossed the line.
The world has long wondered about your brain,
But dissing OPRAH...You must be insane!